C000228809

PENGUIN BOOKS

A THOUSAND MORNINGS

Born in a small town in Ohio, Mary Oliver published her first book of poetry in 1963 at the age of twenty-eight. Over the course of her long career, she received numerous awards. Her fourth book, *American Primitive*, won the Pulitzer Prize for poetry in 1984. She led workshops and held residencies at various colleges and universities, including Bennington College, where she held the Catharine Osgood Foster Chair for Distinguished Teaching. She died in 2019.

MARY OLIVER

A THOUSAND MORNINGS

PENGUIN BOOKS

PENGUIN BOOKS
An imprint of Penguin Random House LLC
penguinrandomhouse.com

First published in the United States of America by Penguin Press,
an imprint of Penguin Random House LLC, 2012
Published in Penguin Books 2013

THE LIBRARY OF CONGRESS HAS CATALOGED THE HARDCOVER EDITION AS FOLLOWS:
Oliver, Mary.
A thousand mornings / Mary Oliver.
p. cm.
ISBN 978-1-59420-477-7 (hc.)
ISBN 978-0-14-312405-4 (pbk.)
I. Title.
PS3565.L5T54 2012
811'.54—dc23   2012027310

Printed in the United States of America
27th Printing

DESIGNED BY AMANDA DEWEY

For
Anne Taylor

CONTENTS

The life that I could still live, I should
live, and the thoughts that I could still
think, I should think.

—C. G. Jung, *The Red Book*

Anything worth thinking about is worth
singing about.

—Bob Dylan, *The Essential Interviews*

A THOUSAND MORNINGS

I GO DOWN TO THE SHORE

I go down to the shore in the morning

and depending on the hour the waves

are rolling in or moving out,

and I say, oh, I am miserable,

what shall—

what should I do? And the sea says

in its lovely voice:

Excuse me, I have work to do.

I HAPPENED TO BE STANDING

I don't know where prayers go,
    or what they do.
Do cats pray, while they sleep
    half-asleep in the sun?
Does the opossum pray as it
    crosses the street?
The sunflowers? The old black oak
    growing older every year?
I know I can walk through the world,
    along the shore or under the trees,
with my mind filled with things
    of little importance, in full
self-attendance. A condition I can't really
    call being alive.
Is a prayer a gift, or a petition,
    or does it matter?
The sunflowers blaze, maybe that's their way.
Maybe the cats are sound asleep. Maybe not.

While I was thinking this I happened to be standing
just outside my door, with my notebook open,
which is the way I begin every morning.
Then a wren in the privet began to sing.

He was positively drenched in enthusiasm,

I don't know why. And yet, why not.

I wouldn't persuade you from whatever you believe

or whatever you don't. That's your business.

But I thought, of the wren's singing, what could this be

    if it isn't a prayer?

So I just listened, my pen in the air.

FOOLISHNESS? NO, IT'S NOT

Sometimes I spend all day trying to count the leaves on a single tree. To do this I have to climb branch by branch and write down the numbers in a little book. So I suppose, from their point of view, it's reasonable that my friends say: what foolishness! She's got her head in the clouds again.

But it's not. Of course I have to give up, but by then I'm half crazy with the wonder of it—the abundance of the leaves, the quietness of the branches, the hopelessness of my effort. And I am in that delicious and important place, roaring with laughter, full of earth-praise.

THE GARDENER

Have I lived enough?

Have I loved enough?

Have I considered Right Action enough, have I
   come to any conclusion?

Have I experienced happiness with sufficient gratitude?

Have I endured loneliness with grace?

I say this, or perhaps I'm just thinking it.
   Actually, I probably think too much.

Then I step out into the garden,
where the gardener, who is said to be a simple man,
   is tending his children, the roses.

AFTER I FALL DOWN THE STAIRS AT THE GOLDEN TEMPLE

For a while I could not remember some word
    I was in need of,
and I was bereaved and said: where are you,
    beloved friend?

IF I WERE

There are lots of ways to dance and to spin, sometimes it just starts my feet first then my entire body, I am spinning no one can see it but it is happening. I am so glad to be alive, I am so glad to be loving and loved. Even if I were close to the finish, even if I were at my final breath, I would be here to take a stand, bereft of such astonishments, but for them.

If I were a Sufi for sure I would be one of the spinning kind.

GOOD-BYE FOX

He was lying under a tree, licking up the shade.

Hello again, Fox, I said.

And hello to you too, said Fox, looking up and
not bounding away.

You're not running away? I said.

Well, I've heard of your conversation about us. News
travels even among foxes, as you might know or not know.

What conversation do you mean?

Some lady said to you, "The hunt is good for the fox."
And you said, "Which fox?"

Yes, I remember. She was huffed.

So you're okay in my book.

Your book! That was in my book, that's the difference
between us.

Yes, I agree. You fuss over life with your clever
words, mulling and chewing on its meaning, while
we just live it.

Oh!

Could anyone figure it out, to a finality? So
why spend so much time trying. You fuss, we live.

And he stood, slowly, for he was old now, and
ambled away.

POEM OF THE ONE WORLD

This morning
the beautiful white heron
was floating along above the water

and then into the sky of this
the one world
we all belong to

where everything
sooner or later
is a part of everything else

which thought made me feel
for a little while
quite beautiful myself.

"Anything worth thinking about is worth
   singing about."

Which is why we have
songs of praise, songs of love, songs
   of sorrow.

Songs to the gods, who have
   so many names.

Songs the shepherds sing, on the
   lonely mountains, while the sheep
      are honoring the grass, by eating it.

The dance-songs of the bees, to tell
   where the flowers, suddenly, in the
      morning light, have opened.

A chorus of many, shouting to heaven,
   or at it, or pleading.

Or that greatest of love affairs, a violin
   and a human body.

And a composer, maybe hundreds of years dead.

I think of Schubert, scribbling on a café
  napkin.
        Thank you, thank you.

THREE THINGS TO REMEMBER

As long as you're dancing, you can
    break the rules.
Sometimes breaking the rules is just
    extending the rules.

Sometimes there are no rules.

HURRICANE

It didn't behave
like anything you had
ever imagined. The wind
tore at the trees, the rain
fell for days slant and hard.
The back of the hand
to everything. I watched
the trees bow and their leaves fall
and crawl back into the earth.
As though, that was that.
This was one hurricane
I lived through, the other one
was of a different sort, and
lasted longer. Then
I felt my own leaves giving up and
falling. *The back of the hand to*
everything. But listen now to what happened
to the actual trees;
toward the end of that summer they
pushed new leaves from their stubbed limbs.
It was the wrong season, yes,
but they couldn't stop. They

looked like telephone poles and didn't
care. And after the leaves came
blossoms. For some things
there are no wrong seasons.
Which is what I dream of for me.

TODAY

Today I'm flying low and I'm
not saying a word.
I'm letting all the voodoos of ambition sleep.

The world goes on as it must,
the bees in the garden rumbling a little,
the fish leaping, the gnats getting eaten.
And so forth.

But I'm taking the day off.
Quiet as a feather.
I hardly move though really I'm traveling
a terrific distance.

Stillness. One of the doors
into the temple.

THE FIRST TIME PERCY CAME BACK

The first time Percy came back

he was not sailing on a cloud.

He was loping along the sand as though

he had come a great way.

"Percy," I cried out, and reached to him—

 those white curls—

but he was unreachable. As music

is present yet you can't touch it.

"Yes, it's all different," he said.

"You're going to be very surprised."

But I wasn't thinking of that. I only

wanted to hold him. "Listen," he said,

"I miss that too.

And now you'll be telling stories

 of my coming back

and they won't be false, and they won't be true,

but they'll be real."

And then, as he used to, he said, "Let's go!"

And we walked down the beach together.

LINES WRITTEN IN THE DAYS
OF GROWING DARKNESS

Every year we have been
witness to it: how the
world descends

into a rich mash, in order that
it may resume.
And therefore
who would cry out

to the petals on the ground
to stay,
knowing as we must,
how the vivacity of *what was* is married

to the vitality of *what will be*?
I don't say
it's easy, but
what else will do

if the love one claims to have for the world
be true?

So let us go on, cheerfully enough,
this and every crisping day,

though the sun be swinging east,
and the ponds be cold and black,
and the sweets of the year be doomed.

BLAKE DYING

He lay
with the pearl of his life under the pillow.

Space shone, cool and silvery,
in the empty cupboards

while he heard in the distance, he said,
the angels singing.

Now and again his white wrists
rose a little above the white sheet.

When death is about to happen
does the body grow heavier, or lighter?

He felt himself growing heavier.
He felt himself growing lighter.

When a man says he hears angels singing
he hears angels singing.

When a man says he hears angels singing,
he hears angels singing.

THE MOCKINGBIRD

All summer
the mockingbird
in his pearl-gray coat
and his white-windowed wings

flies
from the hedge to the top of the pine
and begins to sing, but it's neither
lilting nor lovely,

for he is the thief of other sounds—
whistles and truck brakes and dry hinges
plus all the songs
of other birds in his neighborhood;

mimicking and elaborating,
he sings with humor and bravado,
so I have to wait a long time
for the softer voice of his own life

to come through. He begins
by giving up all his usual flutter
and settling down on the pine's forelock
then looking around

as though to make sure he's alone;
then he slaps each wing against his breast,
where his heart is,
and, copying nothing, begins

easing into it
as though it was not half so easy
as rollicking,
as though his subject now

was his true self,
which of course was as dark and secret
as anyone else's,
and it was too hard—

perhaps you understand—
to speak or to sing it
to anything or anyone
but the sky.

THE MOTH, THE MOUNTAINS,
THE RIVERS

Who can guess the luna's sadness who lives so briefly? Who can guess the impatience of stone longing to be ground down, to be part again of something livelier? Who can imagine in what heaviness the rivers remember their original clarity?

Strange questions, yet I have spent worthwhile time with them. And I suggest them to you also, that your spirit grow in curiosity, that your life be richer than it is, that you bow to the earth as you feel how it actually is, that we—so clever, and ambitious, and selfish, and unrestrained— are only one design of the moving, the vivacious many.

A THOUSAND MORNINGS

All night my heart makes its way
however it can over the rough ground
of uncertainties, but only until night
meets and then is overwhelmed by
morning, the light deepening, the
wind easing and just waiting, as I
too wait (and when have I ever been
disappointed?) for redbird to sing.

AN OLD STORY

Sleep comes its little while. Then I wake
in the valley of midnight or three a.m.
to the first fragrances of spring

which is coming, all by itself, no matter what.
My heart says, what you thought you have you do not have.
My body says, will this pounding ever stop?

My heart says: there, there, be a good student.
My body says: let me up and out, I want to fondle
those soft white flowers, open in the night.

HUM, HUM

1.

One summer afternoon I heard
    a looming, mysterious hum
        high in the air; then came something

like a small planet flying past—
    something

not at all interested in me but on its own
    way somewhere, all anointed with excitement:
        bees, swarming,

not to be held back.

Nothing could hold them back.

2.

Gannets diving.
Black snake wrapped in a tree, our eyes
    meeting.

The grass singing
      as it sipped up the summer rain.
The owl in the darkness, that good darkness
      under the stars.

The child that was myself, that kept running away
      to the also running creek,
to colt's foot and trilliums,
      to the effortless prattle of the birds.

3. SAID THE MOTHER

You are going to grow up
      and in order for that to happen
I am going to have to grow old
      and then I will die, and the blame
will be yours.

4. OF THE FATHER

He wanted a body
      so he took mine.
Some wounds never vanish.

Yet little by little
I learned to love my life.

Though sometimes I had to run hard—
    especially from melancholy—

not to be held back.

5.

I think there ought to be
    a little music here:
        hum, hum.

6.

The resurrection of the morning.
The mystery of the night.
The hummingbird's wings.
The excitement of thunder.
The rainbow in the waterfall.
Wild mustard, that rough blaze of the fields.

The mockingbird, replaying the songs of his
　　neighbors.
The bluebird with its unambitious warble
　　simple yet sufficient.

The shining fish. The beak of the crow.
The new colt who came to me and leaned
　　against the fence
that I might put my hands upon his warm body
　　and know no fear.

Also the words of poets
a hundred or hundreds of years dead—
their words that would not be held back.

7.

Oh the house of denial has thick walls
and very small windows
and whoever lives there, little by little,
will turn to stone.

In those years I did everything I could do
and I did it in the dark—
I mean, without understanding.

I ran away.
I ran away again.
Then, again, I ran away.

They were awfully little, those bees,
and maybe frightened,
yet unstoppably they flew on, somewhere,
to live their life.

Hum, hum, hum.

I HAVE DECIDED

I have decided to find myself a home
in the mountains, somewhere high up
where one learns to live peacefully in
the cold and the silence. It's said that
in such a place certain revelations may
be discovered. That what the spirit
reaches for may be eventually felt, if not
exactly understood. Slowly, no doubt. I'm
not talking about a vacation.

Of course at the same time I mean to
stay exactly where I am.

Are you following me?

WAS IT NECESSARY TO DO IT?

I tell you that ant is very alive!

Look at how he fusses at being stepped on.

GREEN, GREEN IS MY SISTER'S HOUSE

Don't you dare climb that tree
or even try, they said, or you will be
sent away to the hospital of the
very foolish, if not the other one.
And I suppose, considering my age,
it was fair advice.

But the tree is a sister to me, she
lives alone in a green cottage
high in the air and I know what
would happen, she'd clap her green hands,
she'd shake her green hair, she'd
welcome me. Truly

I try to be good but sometimes
a person just has to break out and
act like the wild and springy thing
one used to be. It's impossible not
to remember *wild* and want it back. So

if someday you can't find me you might
look into that tree or—of course
it's possible—under it.

THE INSTANT

Today
one small snake lay, looped and
solitary
in the high grass, it

swirled to look, didn't
like what it saw
and was gone
in two pulses

forward and with no sound at all, only
two taps, in disarray, from
that other shy one,
my heart.

THE WAY OF THE WORLD

The chickens ate all the crickets.
The foxes ate all the chickens.

This morning a friend hauled his
boat to shore and gave me the most
wondrous fish. In its silver scales
it seemed dressed for a wedding.
The gills were pulsing, just above
where shoulders would be, if it had
had shoulders. The eyes were still
looking around, I don't know what
they were thinking.

The chickens ate all the crickets.
The foxes ate all the chickens.

I ate the fish.

EXTENDING THE AIRPORT RUNWAY

The good citizens of the commission
cast their votes
for more of everything.
Very early in the morning

I go out
to the pale dunes, to look over
the empty spaces
of the wilderness.

For something is there,
something is there when nothing is there but itself,
that is not there when anything else is.

Alas,
the good citizens of the commission
have never seen it,

whatever it is,
formless, yet palpable.
Very shining, very delicate.

Very rare.

TIDES

Every day the sea
    blue gray green lavender
pulls away leaving the harbor's
dark-cobbled undercoat

slick and rutted and worm-riddled, the gulls
walk there among old whalebones, the white
    spines of fish blink from the strandy stew
as the hours tick over; and then

far out the faint, sheer
    line turns, rustling over the slack,
the outer bars, over the green-furred flats, over
the clam beds, slippery logs,

barnacle-studded stones, dragging
the shining sheets forward, deepening,
    pushing, wreathing together
wave and seaweed, their piled curvatures

spilling over themselves, lapping
    blue gray green lavender, never

resting, not ever but fashioning shore,
continent, everything.

And here you may find me
on almost any morning
walking along the shore so
    light-footed so casual.

OUT OF THE STUMP ROT, SOMETHING

Out of the stump rot
something
glides forward
that is not a rope,

unless a rope has eyes,
lips,
tongue like a smack of smoke,
body without shoulders.

Thus: the black snake
floating
over the leaves
of the old year

and down to the pond,
to the green just beginning
to fuzzle out of the earth,
also, like smoke.

If you like a prettiness,
don't come here.
Look at pictures instead,
or wait for the daffodils.

This is spring,

by the rattled pond, in the shambled woods,

as spring has always been

and always will be

no matter what we do

in the suburbs.

The matted fur,

the red blood,

the bats unshuttering

their terrible faces,

and black snake

gliding across the field

you think you own.

Long neck, long tail.

Tongue on fire.

Heart of stone.

IN OUR WOODS,
SOMETIMES A RARE MUSIC

Every spring
I hear the thrush singing
in the glowing woods
he is only passing through.
His voice is deep,
then he lifts it until it seems
to fall from the sky.
I am thrilled.

                  I am grateful.

Then, by the end of morning,
he's gone, nothing but silence
out of the tree
where he rested for a night.
And this I find acceptable.
Not enough is a poor life.
But too much is, well, too much.
Imagine Verdi or Mahler
every day, all day.
It would exhaust anyone.

THE MORNING PAPER

Read one newspaper daily (the morning edition
        is the best
for by evening you know that you at least
        have lived through another day)
and let the disasters, the unbelievable
        yet approved decisions,
soak in.

I don't need to name the countries,
        ours among them.

What keeps us from falling down, our faces
        to the ground; ashamed, ashamed?

THE POET COMPARES HUMAN NATURE TO THE OCEAN FROM WHICH WE CAME

The sea can do craziness, it can do smooth,
it can lie down like silk breathing
or toss havoc shoreward; it can give

gifts or withhold all; it can rise, ebb, froth
like an incoming frenzy of fountains, or it can
sweet-talk entirely. As I can too,

and so, no doubt, can you, and you.

ON TRAVELING TO BEAUTIFUL PLACES

Every day I'm still looking for God
and I'm still finding him everywhere,
in the dust, in the flowerbeds.
Certainly in the oceans,
in the islands that lay in the distance
continents of ice, countries of sand
each with its own set of creatures
and God, by whatever name.
How perfect to be aboard a ship with
maybe a hundred years still in my pocket.
But it's late, for all of us,
and in truth the only ship there is
is the ship we are all on
burning the world as we go.

THE MAN WHO HAS MANY ANSWERS

The man who has many answers
is often found
in the theaters of information
where he offers, graciously,
his deep findings.

While the man who has only questions,
to comfort himself, makes music.

LIFE STORY

When I lived under the black oaks
I felt I was made of leaves.
When I lived by Little Sister Pond,
I dreamed I was the feather of the blue heron
left on the shore;
I was the pond lily, my root delicate as an artery,
my face like a star,
my happiness brimming.
Later I was the footsteps that follow the sea.
I knew the tides, I knew the ingredients of the wrack.
I knew the eider, the red-throated loon
with his uplifted beak and his smart eye.
I felt I was the tip of the wave,
the pearl of water on the eider's glossy back.
No, there's no escaping, nor would I want to escape
this outgo, this foot-loosening, this solution
to gravity and a single shape.
Now I am here, later I will be there.
I will be that small cloud, staring down at the water,
the one that stalls, that lifts its white legs, that

    looks like a lamb.

"FOR I WILL CONSIDER MY DOG PERCY"

For I will consider my dog Percy.

For he was made small but brave of heart.

For if he met another dog he would kiss her in kindness.

For when he slept he snored only a little.

For he could be silly and noble in the same moment.

For when he spoke he remembered the trumpet and when
   he scratched he struck the floor like a drum.

For he ate only the finest food and drank only the
   purest of water, yet would nibble of dead fish also.

For he came to me impaired and therefore certain of
   short life, yet thoroughly rejoiced in each day.

For he took his medicines without argument.

For he played easily with the neighborhood's Bull
   Mastiff.

For when he came upon mud he splashed through it.

*For he was an instrument for the children to learn
benevolence upon.*

For he listened to poems as well as love-talk.

For when he sniffed it was as if he were being
pleased by every part of the world.

For when he sickened he rallied as many times as
he could.

For he was a mixture of gravity and waggery.

For we humans can seek self-destruction in ways
he never dreamed of.

For he took actions both cunning and reckless, yet
refused always to offer himself to be admonished.

For his sadness though without words was
understandable.

For there was nothing sweeter than his peace
     when at rest.

For there was nothing brisker than his life when
     in motion.

For he was of the tribe of Wolf.

For when I went away he would watch for me at
     the window.

For he loved me.

For he suffered before I found him, and never
     forgot it.

For he loved Anne.

For when he lay down to enter sleep he did not argue
     about whether or not God made him.

For he could fling himself upside down and laugh
     a true laugh.

For he loved his friend Ricky.

For he would dig holes in the sand and then let
Ricky lie in them.

For often I see his shape in the clouds and this is
a continual blessing.

VARANASI

Early in the morning we crossed the ghat,

where fires were still smoldering,

and gazed, with our Western minds, into the Ganges.

A woman was standing in the river up to her waist;

she was lifting handfuls of water and spilling it

over her body, slowly and many times,

as if until there came some moment

of inner satisfaction between her own life and the river's.

Then she dipped a vessel she had brought with her

and carried it filled with water back across the ghat,

no doubt to refresh some shrine near where she lives,

for this is the holy city of Shiva, maker

of the world, and this is his river.

I can't say much more, except that it all happened

in silence and peaceful simplicity, and something that felt

like the bliss of a certainty and a life lived

in accordance with that certainty.

I must remember this, I thought, as we fly back

to America.

Pray God I remember this.

NOTE

The poem "For I Will Consider My Dog Percy" is obviously derivative of Christopher Smart's poem "For I Will Consider My Cat Jeoffry." It is in no way an imitation except in style. Jeoffry wins entirely. But for a few days I simply stood upon the shoulders of that wondrous poem and began to think about Percy.

The lines in italics, except for the exchange of names and altering of verb tense from present to past, are Christopher Smart's own, and in that way are acknowledged to be so.

M. O.

ACKNOWLEDGMENTS

My thanks to the editors of the following publications in which the listed poems previously appeared, some in slightly different form.

APPALACHIA: "Foolishness? No, It's Not"; "The Instant"

BARK: "The First Time Percy Came Back"

FIVE POINTS: "*Hum, Hum*"; "Poem of the One World"

THE NEW YORK TIMES: "Lines Written in the Days of Growing Darkness"

ORION: "Life Story"

PARABOLA: "I Go Down to the Shore"; "After I Fall Down the Stairs at the Golden Temple"; "If I Were"; "And Bob Dylan Too"; "The Morning Paper"

PORTLAND: "Today"

SHENANDOAH: "Out of the Stump Rot Something"

WILDERNESS: "Extending the Airport Runway"

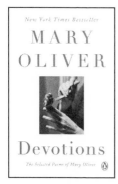
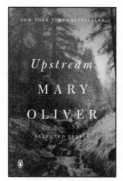
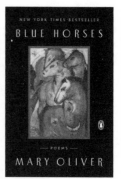

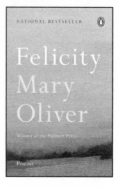